LEARN ABOUT VALUES

LOYALTY

by Cynthia A. Klingel

The Child's World®

Published in the United States of America by The Child's World®
1980 Lookout Drive • Mankato, MN 56003-1705 • 800-599-READ • www.childsworld.com

The Child's World®: Mary Berendes, Publishing Director; Katherine Stevenson, Editor
The Design Lab: Kathy Petelinsek, Art Director; Julia Goozen, Design and Page Production

Photo Credits: © Ariel Skelley/Corbis: cover; © Brand X Pictures: 9; © David M. Budd Photography: 7, 11, 13, 17; © iStockphoto.com/Jane Norton: 21; © iStockphoto.com/Rob Friedman: 5; © Larry Bones/Getty Images: 15; © P Deliss/Godong/Corbis: 19

Library of Congress Cataloging-in-Publication Data
Klingel, Cynthia Fitterer.
  Loyalty / by Cynthia A. Klingel.
    p. cm. — (Learn about values)
  ISBN 978-1-59296-672-1 ISBN 1-59296-672-1 (library bound: alk. paper)
  1. Loyalty—Juvenile literature. 2. Values—Juvenile literature. I. Title. II. Series.
  BJ1533.L8K55 2006
  179'.9—dc22   2006000974

CONTENTS

What Is Loyalty?

Have you ever stuck up for someone or something? Maybe you had a friend who needed help. Perhaps you had a **favorite** sports team no one else liked. Loyalty is believing in something or someone and standing up for them. Loyalty is being **faithful**.

4

Loyalty is being faithful to others—even sports teams!

Loyalty to Friends

Maybe your friend got in an **argument** with another girl. The other girl said something mean to your friend. You showed loyalty to your friend by standing up for her. Maybe the other girl did not like that! But you showed your friend she can count on you.

Loyalty means sticking up for your friends.

Loyalty to Your Team

Maybe you are on a baseball team. You do not always win.
Sometimes the other kids do not play well. Sometimes you do not
play well, either! But you stay loyal to your team. You cheer during
the team's games. You tell everyone they did a good job.

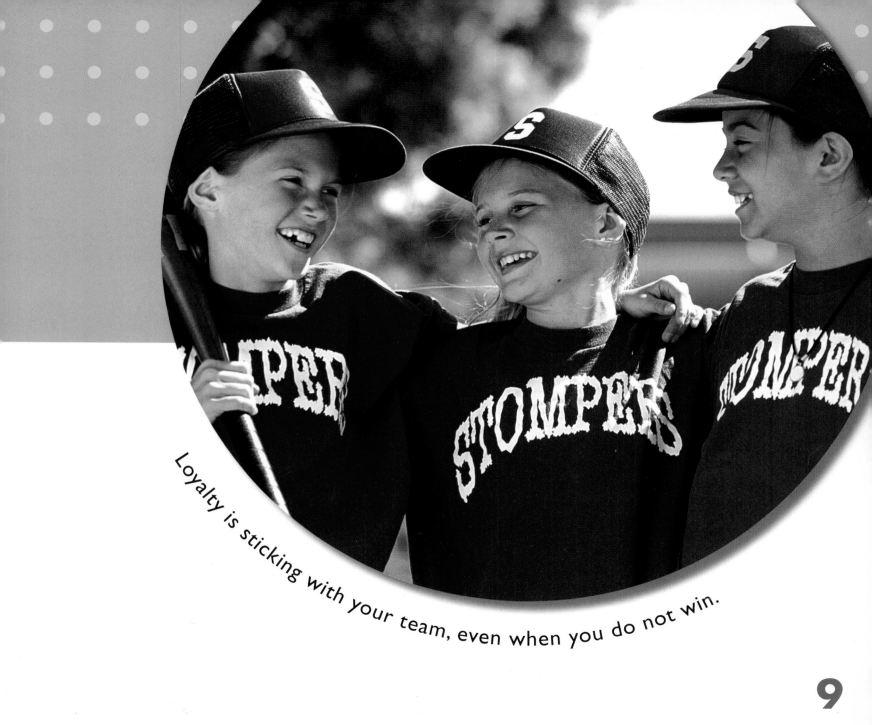

Loyalty is sticking with your team, even when you do not win.

Loyalty to Your School

You like your school. The teachers do a good job. The other kids are great. Maybe some other schools have nicer buildings. Maybe they have nicer playgrounds. But you are loyal to your own school. You tell other people how much you like it.

You can show loyalty by telling your friends they did well.

Loyalty to Your Family

You and your sister are playing a game with other kids. Your sister makes a big mistake. Everyone gets mad at her. They say mean things. Your sister runs home. The other kids keep playing without her. You want to keep playing, too. But you feel bad for your sister. You want to be with her. You show loyalty to your sister by going home.

Loyalty to your family means being there when they need help.

Loyalty to Your Neighborhood

You like to visit your friend's house. She lives in a nicer neighborhood than yours. Your neighborhood sometimes gets messy. You show loyalty to your neighborhood by helping to keep it clean. You follow the rules and laws. You think of ways to make your neighborhood even better.

Loyalty can make your neighborhood a great place to live!

Loyalty to Your Country

You are proud of your country. You take off your hat when you see the flag. You put your hand over your heart when you sing the **anthem**. You feel loyal to your country. Loyalty to your country is called **patriotism**.

People show loyalty to their countries in many different ways.

Loyalty to Your Beliefs

People have lots of different beliefs. They have different beliefs about the world. They have different ideas about how things should be done. Some people might agree with your beliefs. Other people might not. It is OK for people to believe in different things. You can show loyalty to your own beliefs by standing by them.

18

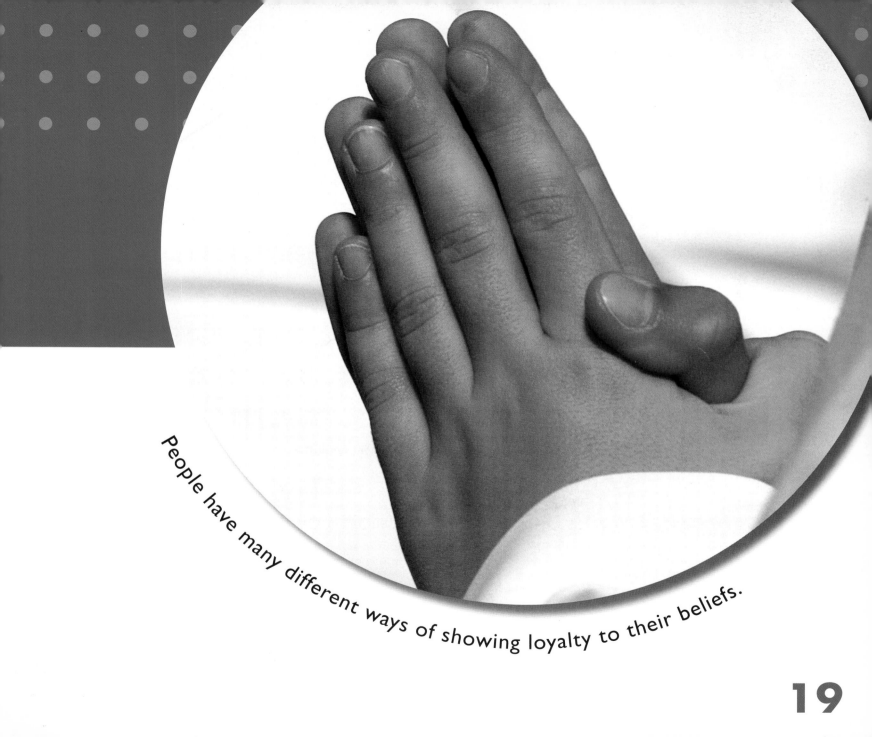

People have many different ways of showing loyalty to their beliefs.

Loyalty Can Be Hard!

Being loyal is not always easy. But it lets people know who you are. It lets them know what you believe in. It lets them know that you care. People will trust you when they know you are loyal.

Loyalty helps us make strong friendships.

glossary

anthem
An anthem is a national song.

argument
Having an argument means disagreeing in an angry way.

faithful
When you are faithful to something, you stick with it.

favorite
When you like something best, it is your favorite.

patriotism
Patriotism is a feeling of love and respect for your country.

books

San Souci, Robert D. *The Faithful Friend*. New York: Aladdin, 1999.

Turner, Pamela S. *Hachiko: The True Story of a Loyal Dog*. New York: Houghton Mifflin, 2004.

web sites

Visit our Web page for links about character education and values:
http://www.childsworld.com/links

Note to parents, teachers, and librarians:
We routinely check our Web links to make sure they're safe,
active sites—so encourage your readers to check them out!

index

about the author

Cynthia A. Klingel is Director of Curriculum and Instruction for a school district in Minnesota. She enjoys reading, writing, gardening, traveling, and spending time with friends and family.

24